James Ross Snowden

The Coins of the Bible and it´s monetary Terms

James Ross Snowden

The Coins of the Bible and it´s monetary Terms

ISBN/EAN: 9783743356962

Manufactured in Europe, USA, Canada, Australia, Japa

Cover: Foto ©Lupo / pixelio.de

Manufactured and distributed by brebook publishing software
(www.brebook.com)

James Ross Snowden

The Coins of the Bible and it´s monetary Terms

THE

COINS OF THE BIBLE,

AND ITS

MONEY TERMS.

BY

JAMES ROSS SNOWDEN, A.M.,

AUTHOR OF

"COINS OF ALL NATIONS," "MEDALLIC MEMORIALS OF WASHINGTON, NATIONAL MEDALS," &c., &c.

ENLARGED EDITION.

PHILADELPHIA:

PRESBYTERIAN BOARD OF PUBLICATION,

No. 1334 CHESTNUT STREET.

ADVERTISEMENT.

A FEW years ago the writer made some remarks to a Sabbath-school with which he was connected, and exhibited specimens of some of the Coins mentioned in the Bible, namely, a denarius, or "penny;" a shekel, a silver stater, and a lepton, or "widow's mite." There was present on that occasion a clergyman, at whose request the writer prepared a series of articles on the same subject, which were published in the "*Sabbath-school Visitor.*"

In compliance with the repeated request of the same gentleman, and other clergymen and laymen, the writer has arranged these articles, and with several additional chapters, and some introductory remarks, they are presented to the public in the present form.

1 *

As the articles were originally written for a Sabbath-school paper, so now, this little work is mainly intended to be used as a Sabbath-school book. The writer begs to express the hope that its pages will give useful information to youthful inquirers after truth ; and that the statements and tables herein presented, will be found valuable to all readers of the sacred Scriptures into whose hands it may come, and thus advance the interests of our beloved Zion.

J. R. S.

NOTE.

The first edition of this work being exhausted, and a new one called for, the author has availed himself of the opportunity to make some additions to it. The book having been stereotyped it was deemed expedient to insert the chief part of the new matter as *notes* to the text. A few alterations are however made in the body of the work ; and a new chapter, on the Parable of the Talents is added.

J. R. S.

December 8, 1866.

CONTENTS.

CHAPTER VI.

CHAPTER VII.

CHAPTER VIII.

CHAPTER IX.

CHAPTER X.

CHAPTER XI.

CHAPTER XII.

CHAPTER XIII.

INTRODUCTORY CHAPTER.

EXCHANGES of goods and merchandize were the original manner of commerce, and of business transactions. There was no buying, in a proper sense, until money was invented. But such exchanges, or barter of one article for another, being very inconvenient, the necessity of having some circulating medium, or measure of value, arose at a very early period of the world's history.

It is well known that cattle or oxen were at first used for the purposes of currency; the possession of these animals constituted the principal wealth of individuals. Thus, the wealth of the patriarch Job, before and after his wonderful trial, is stated in the number of his cattle. They were the standard by which the value of other articles of a more variable character was regulated.

Homer, who wrote about nine hundred years before the time of our Saviour, mentions the use of cattle as a medium of exchange; he represents one of his heroes as having given his golden armour, worth a hundred oxen, for the brazen armour of another worth only nine oxen. So, also the ancient Romans derived their term *pecunia* (money) from the word *pecus*, which means cattle; and their most ancient coins have upon them the figure of an ox.*

In the course of time, as society advanced and commerce increased, the precious metals, namely, gold and silver, and also copper and brass, were introduced as a substitute for cattle. Gold and silver, it is believed, were the earliest metals discovered. Possessing in an eminent degree, all the properties which peculiarly fit them for a circulating medium, their use as such has been adopted, and continued by all the civilized nations of the earth.

The period when coined money, or pieces

* See note 1, page 79.

of gold and silver, or copper and brass, with devices stamped upon them, were introduced, is involved in some obscurity. The best authorities place the time about seven centuries before the Christian era. But for ages previous to any actual coinage, gold and silver were used as money by weight. Thus, it is said of the patriarch Abraham, about 1918 years B. C., that he "was very rich in cattle, in silver, and in gold." Gen. xiii. 2. And afterwards, namely, 1860 years B. C., on the death of his beloved wife Sarah, he purchased the field of Machpelah for a burial-place: the price of which was paid in silver by weight. "And Abraham hearkened unto Ephron; and Abraham weighed to Ephron the silver which he had named in the audience of the sons of Heth, four hundred shekels of silver, current with the merchant." Gen. xxiii. 16. The shekel was a weight, and is derived from a Hebrew word which means to weigh. It was not a *coin* until several hundred years afterwards; as will be shown in the chapter devoted to the word Shekel.

It is worthy of remark here, that among the Greeks and the Romans, as well as the Jews, the same names were used for weights and coins. A want of attention to this fact has led some writers into an error as to the time when coins, or single pieces of silver or gold, were made. As already said, the best authorities put the time of the earliest coinage at about seven centuries before Christ.

There is a difference of opinion as to the locality where the first coins were struck. Some authorities give that honour to the island of Ægina, in Greece; whilst others assign it to the city of Miletus in Asia Minor. The latter being a colony from Greece, the art may be said to be purely Grecian; and it is quite certain that the coinage of both places, of which there are many specimens extant, were so nearly alike in execution as to place them very nearly side by side at the origin of the invention.

The coins struck at this early period were extremely rude, and contained no letters or symbols, other than the one device upon the principal side. From time to time improvements were made, by placing the initial letter of the country where they were issued, and sometimes the entire name. After that, a device in relief for the reverse or opposite side was adopted; and subsequently a *legend*, which, though abbreviated and sometimes indefinite, affords some assistance in ascertaining the country and period of issue. At a later period, at the time of Philip and Alexander, the portrait of the sovereign had its place upon the coinage.

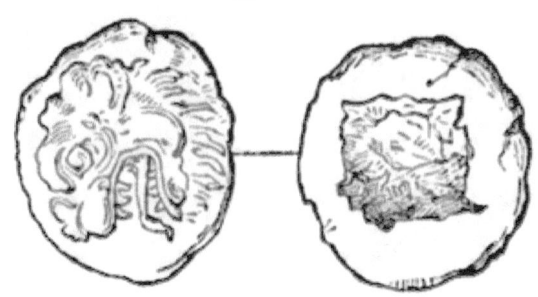

(GOLD STATER OF MILETUS.)

But whilst it is doubtful whether the first coinage of money was executed at Ægina, or Miletus, it seems to be pretty well settled that the first gold coins were made at the latter place. We present herewith a fac-simile representation of the *Stater* of Miletus, the

2

first gold coin, so far as our information extends, ever struck. It has the Lion's head on the *obverse*, or principal side, and the punch mark on the *reverse*.

At this early period the impressions upon the coins were made by a hammer and punch. The piece of metal to be coined was first fashioned into a semi-bullet shape; this being placed upon the face of the die, the punch was applied to it, and struck with a hammer.[1]

After some centuries, other appliances were used; and devices and inscriptions were introduced upon the reverse as well as the obverse of the coins. Without going into a statement of the various changes and advancements in coinage which were made, we may state generally that the principles involved in their execution were the same as above mentioned, until the introduction of the instrument which we illustrate in the annexed engraving.

[1] Coins of all Nations; by J. R. Snowden. Published by J. B. Lippincott & Co., 1860. To this work we refer our readers for further details on this, and other points connected with the subject of coinage.

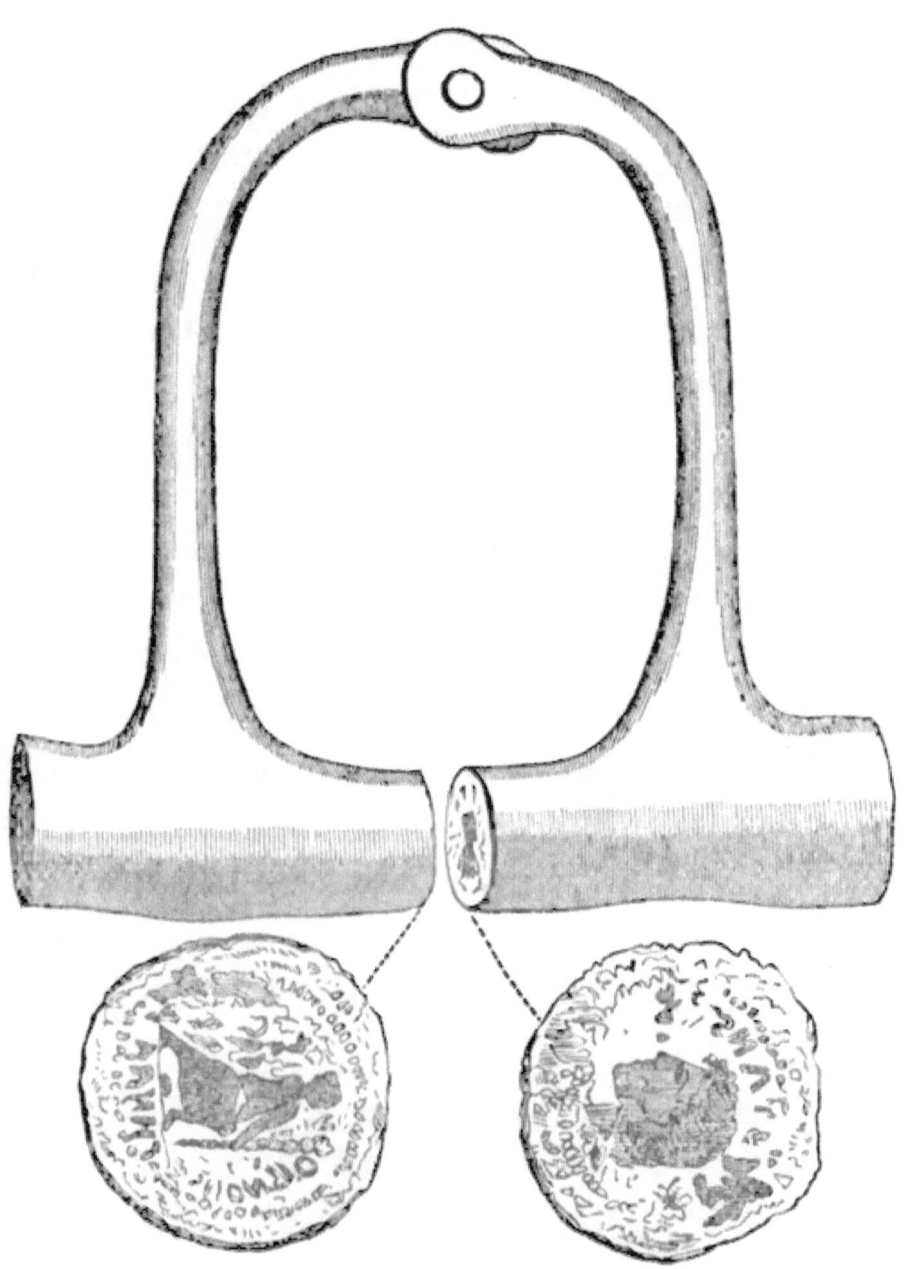

AN ANCIENT COINING PRESS.

We cannot say with certainty when this instrument was invented. The one here represented was used by the Emperor Constans, who reigned from A. D. 337 to 350. On the obverse die, the letters STANS are still visible. The reverse has a Victory, with a trophy and a palm branch.

In 1553, the mill and screw, an invention of French origin was introduced, and was continued until a recent period. It is now used for striking medals which require repeated blows to produce the high relief which generally characterizes these works of art.

The coining press now used, was invented in 1833, by Thonnelier, a Frenchman, and was soon after put in practice in the Mint at Paris. It was introduced into the Mint of the United States, at Philadelphia, in March, 1836.

A representation of the Steam Coining-Press, now in use in the United States Mint, at Philadelphia, is on the opposite page.

This invention is an amazing advance upon the hammer and punch of the ancients. It

A STEAM-COINING PRESS.

is probably the nearest approach to perfection, in regard to both accuracy and speed that it is possible to accomplish. Each press will strike from sixty to ninety pieces per minute, and it requires the attendance of but one person to supply the blanks or planchets from which the coins are made.

These presses are one of the chief objects of interest to the visitor to the Mint. The labour of attending them is so inconsiderable that women are employed therein. They can perform the work as well as men; and it is commendable in this National Institution that women are thus employed, and also in the delicate and important operation of adjusting the weights of the coins to the standard required by law.

COINS OF THE BIBLE.

CHAPTER I.

The Penny.

" And they brought unto him a penny." Matt. xxii. 19.

WE propose, for the information of our young readers, to say a few words about the coins, or pieces of money, which are mentioned in the Holy Scriptures. These coins are not only interesting memorials of antiquity, but they illustrate and confirm the historical references which are made in the sacred text; and so far as their devices and inscriptions can speak to us, they will be found to corroborate its authenticity. Whilst the truths of the gospel should be received with a child-like confidence and reliance, it is interesting to know that even in some of the most minute details, the narratives of the inspired penmen are shown to be confirmed by the coins of that period.*

The engraving at the head of this article presents a picture of the "penny" of the New Testament. It is taken from a fine specimen preserved in the Cabinet of the National Mint in Philadelphia.

Most of our readers, no doubt, have supposed that the "penny," referred to in the text above cited, was a copper coin like our cent; but it is not so; it was a silver coin, called *denarion* by the Greeks, *denarius* by the Romans; and was, at the time of our Saviour's ministry, equal in value to about fifteen cents of our money. It has on the obverse, or principal side, the portrait of Tiberius Cæsar, with the following legend or inscription, TI. CÆSAR. DIVI. AUG. F. AUGUS-

* See note 2, page 80.

TUS. Which may be translated thus: Tiberius
Cæsar Augustus, son of the divine Augustus.
From this we learn the propriety of our Lord's
inquiry, "Whose is this image and superscription?" "And they say unto him, Cæsar's." Matt. xxii. 20, 21. The reverse, or
other side, has a picture or representation of
a female figure seated, with a *hasta* or spear
in her right hand, and an olive branch in the
left. The legend expresses one of the Emperor's titles: PONTIF. MAXIM. *Pontifex maxi-
mus*, that is, Chief Priest, or Pontiff. This
female figure represents Rome; and as she
holds the spear, a weapon of war, in her *right*
hand, and the olive branch, the symbol of
peace, in her *left*, it shows that she prefers
war to peace. The history of Rome exhibits
the truth of this representation. It may interest our readers in this connection to notice,
that the American eagle, which is placed on
the principal coins of our country, holds in
his *right* talon the olive branch of peace, and
in his *left*, the arrows of war, to show that
our country prefers peace to war.

The denarius, or "penny" of Tiberius, which we have described, was a very common coin in the Roman empire, and has been found in most of the countries once under its dominion. Tiberius Cæsar reigned from the year A. D. 14, to A. D. 37; that is to say, during the whole period of our Lord's public ministry. Hence we may reasonably infer that the coin, which the Pharisees and Herodians brought to him, was of this kind. Having the image and superscription of Cæsar upon it, it furnished the Saviour with an opportunity to inculcate the duty of obedience to the civil magistrates, and to the laws of the country, and to teach, that due worship and service should at the same time be rendered to the great Creator of all things. "Render, therefore," says he, "unto Cæsar, the things which are Cæsar's, and unto God, the things that are God's," ver. 21.

When those, who "took counsel how they might entangle him in his talk," heard these words, they went their way astonished and confounded. And thus will it ever be with all who exalt their own wisdom above his, or refuse to acknowledge his authority, and to accept of him as their Teacher and Redeemer.

CHAPTER II.

The Penny.

" And when he had agreed with the labourers for a penny a day, he sent them into his vineyard." Matt. xx. 2.

A PENNY a day seems a small compensation for a labourer; but we have, in the previous chapter, seen that the coin in question was not the penny of the present day, but was a *denarius*, a silver coin, the intrinsic value of which was fifteen cents. This gives one a better idea of the value of labour at that time. And it shows that the good Samaritan was more liberal and generous than the usual reading of the text in Luke x. 35, would indicate. He gave the poor man that fell among thieves two silver coins of the value

of thirty cents. We have reason to believe
that silver was at that period ten times as
valuable as it is at present: in other words,
thirty cents then would buy as much as three
dollars would now. It thus appears that the
Samaritan, besides the other valuable things,
wine and oil, which he bestowed upon the in-
jured man, gave the "host" money enough
to pay the boarding of his guest for some
time, perhaps for several weeks, because this
interesting event happened in the hilly country of Judea, between Jerusalem and Jericho,
where the charges at the inn were probably
quite moderate. Thus a liberal provision was
made for the intervening time which would
elapse before this benevolent man would return from Jerusalem. And in case he should
be delayed in his return, he said to the inn-
keeper, "Take care of this man, and whatsoever thou spendest more, when I come again
I will repay thee." This generous and neigh-
bourly conduct of the good Samaritan our
Lord commends, with the injunction, "Go,
and do thou likewise," ver. 37.

3

The ointment with which Mary anointed our Saviour, is said to have been "very costly," John xii. 3, and "very precious," Mark xiv. 3. "Some had indignation within themselves, and murmured against her," because the ointment might have been sold for more than *three hundred pence*, and the money given to the poor, Mark xiv. 4, 5. The propriety of saying that it was very costly, and very precious, appears very clearly when we ascertain that the price at which it was said that it might have been sold, was equal to forty-five dollars of our money. Mary's offering was therefore a valuable one intrinsically; but much more so as she wrought "a good work, which is spoken of throughout the whole world as a memorial" of her love and devotion to her Saviour, ver. 9.

Again, when the 5000 persons were miraculously fed, we are told that the disciples asked, "Shall we go and buy two hundred pennyworth (*denarii*) of bread, and give them to eat?" Mark vi. 37.

The present value of the penny is about two

cents. We must caution our readers against the popular error of using the words *penny* and *cent*, as equal terms. They belong to different systems of accounts and coinage, and are of different values, and therefore have no analogy with each other.

It would seem to be very unreasonable to talk of feeding such a multitude with four hundred cents worth of bread. But when we know that two hundred pence were equal to thirty dollars of our money, we can readily understand how, with that sum bread enough might have been purchased not only to enable "every one of them to take a little," John vi. 7; but if the proportionate value is considered, the money would have bought a loaf of bread for each one of the great multitude that were there assembled. The great Master of the feast, however, preferred to feed them by his creative power, and thus the five barley loaves, and the two small fishes, were miraculously increased; "and they did all eat and were filled; and they took up twelve baskets full of the fragments." Mark vi. 42, 43.

It is difficult to determine with accuracy the relative value of money in different periods of the world. The pieces of the same denomination, coined at different times, greatly varied in weight and in fineness, or in the proportion of pure silver to the alloy of base metal used in the coinage. The denarius of Tiberius weighed about sixty grains; and contained about ninety per cent. of silver, and ten per cent. of alloy; and was worth, as we have seen, about fifteen cents; but as the Roman empire declined, the denarius was diminished in weight and fineness, until at length it fell to about the value of six cents. It was perhaps on the model of this reduced denarius that the English penny was established. The pound sterling as originally constituted in England, and up to about A. D. 1300, was composed of *a troy pound weight of silver*. As there are 5760 grains in a troy pound, and as the penny is the two hundred and fortieth part of a pound sterling, it will be seen that the penny of our English ancestors weighed twenty-four grains : from which comes the term "penny-weight." At the present mint value of silver, namely 122½ cents per ounce—twenty-four grains, or one penny-weight, is worth six cents: but as one pound troy of silver, is now in England coined into three pounds and six shillings sterling, the weight of the penny would be only about seven grains. This being too small for a coin, the copper penny has been substituted for the silver penny. The Roman term is still preserved in the English money of account of pounds, shillings, and pence; thus £. s. d. (*Libra, Sestertius, Denarius.*) From these considerations it would appear that the translation of the word *denarius* into *penny*, is legitimate and proper in one sense, although it gives an incorrect idea of the *value* of that ancient coin.

We have thus endeavoured to show that it is useful, as well as interesting, to learn something of the value of the *denarius*, inasmuch as it serves to render more clear several passages in the sacred writings.

3 *

CHAPTER III.

The Silver Stater.

GRYPUS.

" And when they were come to Capernaum, they that received tribute-money came to Peter, and said, Doth not your
Master pay tribute? He saith, Yes." Matt. xvii. 24, 25
" Go thou to the sea, and cast a hook, and take up the fish
that first cometh up; and when thou hast opened his mouth,
thou shalt find a piece of money: that take, and give unto
them for me and thee." Ver. 27.

THE piece of money here referred to, is the
silver *stater;** otherwise called a tetradrachm,
that is to say, four drachmas. It is a Greek
coin of the Syrian series. It weighs 250
grains, and being of the fineness of about 95
per cent., its value, at the Mint price of silver,

* Note 3, page 82.

is about sixty-seven cents.   When the shekel
had become obsolete, the stater being nearest
to it in value circulated in its stead.   At
length it was superseded by the money of the
conquering Romans.

The engravings given with this chapter will
afford our readers a good idea of this coin.
They are both staters; one is a coin of
Antiochus Epiphanes; and the other of
Antiochus Grypus (*Grups*, signifies aquiline)
from the curved shape of his nose.   The
obverse on each presents the head of the
king.   On one of the *reverses* Jupiter is represented seated, holding a figure of Victory
in his right hand, and the hasta or spear in
his left.   On the other *reverse* Jupiter standing, with a crescent on his head, holding a

EPIPHANES.

spear and supporting a star. The titles on both are the same—*Basileos Antiochou Epiphanous*—(Money) of King Antiochus the Illustrious. The same title, with similar devices, first appeared on the coins of the first king of that name, who was so famous for his wars with the Jews; but the epithet, "a vile person," which was given to him by the prophet Daniel more than four hundred years before he was born, agrees better with his true character. Dan. xi. 21. Polybius, who wrote in the time of this prince, says he should rather be called Epimanes, or the madman. As his life was one of wickedness, impiety, and cruelty, so his death, as is recorded in the book of Maccabees, was an awful one. 2 Mac. ix. 9.

At the time of our Saviour's mission, the stater we have described was in circulation in Judea; and it seems, as above stated, to have been taken interchangeably with the Jewish shekel. The "tribute" mentioned in the text, was the *didrachm;* and this was equal to the *half-shekel*, which each Jew above the age of twenty years, was required to pay towards the expenses of maintaining the services of the sanctuary. Exod. xxxviii. 26. And hence the stater in the fish's mouth, being equal to *two* half-shekels, was sufficient to pay for Peter as well as for Christ. "Thou shalt find a piece of money (stater,) that take and give unto them for me and thee."

The payment of the half-shekel, which at first was applied to the service of the Tabernacle, and afterwards to the Temple, was not compulsory. The money did not go to Cæsar, or the civil magistrate, like the denarius, or penny, referred to by our Lord on a subsequent occasion. Matt. xxii. 19. And it was at first, we learn, only collected occasionally, as it was wanted for the service of the sanctuary, although it afterwards became an annual payment. Christ in his inquiries and remarks to Peter, shows that, as he was the Son of God, and therefore the Lord of the Temple, he was under no obligation to pay the *didrachm*, (translated "tribute.") Lest, however, any should take offence at his refusal, as if he did not regard the temple-worship, or had come to destroy the law, he would waive his privilege and pay it. And this he did in a way which showed he was "the Christ, the Son of the living God."

This miracle testifies that although he was externally poor, yet he was Lord over nature; and even the fishes of the sea were under his control, and subservient to his requirements. It may be admitted that it is no absolute miracle that a coin should be found in a fish's mouth: but by whatever means the piece of money was lodged there, Omniscience alone could discover it there, and Omnipotence insure its being brought to Peter's hook. Had he chosen to exercise his power, all the treasures of the land and sea might have been placed at his feet. But he came into the world to be a suffering Saviour and Redeemer. May your hearts, my readers, go forth in love and gratitude to Him who, "though he was rich, yet for your sakes he became poor, that ye through his poverty might be rich."

CHAPTER IV.

The Shekel.

" Then one of the twelve, called Judas Iscariot, went unto the chief priests, and said unto them, ' What will ye give me, and I will deliver him unto you ?' And they covenanted with him for thirty pieces of silver." Matt. xxvi. 14, 15.

THE silver pieces that were given to Judas, we have reason to believe, were *shekels.* In the original text, no particular *coins* are mentioned; but a Greek word is used (*arguria*) which means "*pieces of silver.*" The *shekel* was originally a weight. The first form in which money was used by the Jews, and by all other nations of which we have any knowledge, was that of pieces of metal without any regular shape, or any marks or devices upon them. The precious metals, namely, gold and silver, passed by weight. Thus it is said of the purchase made by Abraham, of the cave and field of Machpelah, "And Abraham hearkened unto Ephron, and Abraham weighed to Ephron the silver which he had named in the audience of the sons of Heth, four hundred shekels of silver, current with the merchant." Gen. xxiii. 16.

In paying for the field of Hanameel, the prophet Jeremiah "weighed him the money, even seventeen shekels of silver; and subscribed the evidence and sealed it, and took witnesses, and weighed him the money in the balances." Jer. xxxii. 9, 10. The weight of a shekel was a little less than one half of an ounce troy; the term "current with the merchant," probably refers to the purity of the silver, which was about ninety-five per cent. fine; the consequent value of the shekel of silver was fifty-eight cents of our money. The weight and value of the shekel will be further noticed in a subsequent chapter.

It is to be noted that the shekel was not a

coin in Abraham's time, nor during the entire period embraced in the Old Testament. It first appears as a coin in the time of the Maccabees, who lived about 140 B. C. The amount of silver in the coin is the same as was contained in the piece of silver denominated a shekel: and, therefore, took the name of a shekel. The engraving at the commencement of this chapter gives a faithful representation of one of these coins. It will be seen that on one side is the golden cup that had manna, (see Exod. xvi. 33; and Heb. ix. 4,) with the inscription, in old Hebrew character, "SHEKEL OF ISRAEL;" on the other side appears Aaron's rod that budded, with the legend, in the same character, "JERUSALEM THE HOLY." This specimen is in the Cabinet of the National Mint at Philadelphia, and is one of the most rare and interesting coins in the collection.

To the betrayal of the Saviour by Judas, reference appears to be made by the prophet Zechariah, "So they weighed for my price thirty pieces of silver;" "and the Lord said unto me, Cast it to the potter. A goodly price that I was prized at of them." Zech. xi. 12, 13. By the law, thirty pieces of silver was the price of a servant or slave. Exod. xxi. 32. And it appears to have been a part of the office of the priests to put a value upon devoted things. Lev. xxvii. 8. The events recorded in the New Testament fulfil these and other wonderful prophecies respecting the Messiah. He "made himself of no reputation, and took upon him the form of a servant." Phil. ii. 7. The valuation was made by the priests. "What will ye give me, and I will deliver him unto you?" says Judas to the priests. "And they covenanted with him for thirty pieces of silver." Matt. xxvi. 15. "Then Judas which had betrayed him, when he saw that he was condemned, repented himself, and brought again the thirty pieces of silver to the chief priests and elders." "And he cast down the pieces of silver in the temple and departed, and went and hanged himself." "And the chief priests took the silver pieces and said, It is not lawful for to put them into the treasury, because it is the price of blood." "And they took counsel and bought with them the potter's field to bury strangers in." Matt. xxvii. 3, 5, 6, and 7.

Thus does the shekel—one of the thirty pieces of silver—become a lasting memorial of the betrayal of our Saviour, and of the fulfilment of the Scriptures. "The son of man came, not to be ministered unto, but to minister, and to give his life a ransom for many."

The contemplation of these amazing events should fill every heart with love and gratitude to the blessed Redeemer, "In whom we have redemption through his blood, the forgiveness of sins, according to the riches of his grace."

CHAPTER V.

The Denarius of Vespasian recording the conquest of Judea.

"And his disciples came to him, for to show him the buildings of the temple. And Jesus said unto them, See ye not all these things? Verily I say unto you, there shall not be left here one stone upon another that shall not be thrown down." Matt. xxiv. 1, 2.

THE pictures at the head of this chapter represent a denarius, struck to commemorate the destruction of the city of Jerusalem. It is a silver coin, weighing about fifty-two grains. It contains nearly seventy-eight per cent. of pure silver, and is of the value of about eleven cents of our money. A specimen of this coin is preserved in the cabinet of the Mint at Philadelphia. The *obverse* has a portrait of the Emperor Vespasian, with an inscription giving his name and titles. We may here note that the name *Augustus*—AUG.—on this coin, was assumed by Tiberius as an official title, and was continued by his successors. The *reverse* presents a female captive, with her hands bound before her, standing near a palm-tree, with the legend IVDAEA DEVICTA, Judea vanquished.

The destruction of Jerusalem was foretold by our Saviour, about forty years before that remarkable event happened. These prophecies are chiefly recorded in the twenty-fourth chapter of St. Matthew. They related not only to the destruction of the city and of the temple and of the Jews, but they contained a timely warning to the Christians in Jerusalem, by which they knew, from the signs of the times, that desolation was near at hand, and that they should consult their safety and flee into the mountains. This the disciples were enabled to do, in consequence of the de-

4 *

lays by the Romans in carrying on the war, and in making the actual investment of the city.

Vespasian was Emperor of Rome from A. D. 69 to A. D. 79. He had previously, under the orders of the emperor Nero, acted as governor of Judea, and commanded the army which invaded that country. Many of the cities of Palestine had surrendered to him; and he had made preparations to besiege the city of Jerusalem. But he was called away by the civil wars between Otho and Vitellius; and on the death of the latter,—who fell by the hands of his own soldiers—Vespasian was declared Emperor by the army. The city of Jerusalem was not actually besieged until after Vespasian was confirmed in the empire, and Titus, his son, was sent by him to command the forces in Judea. By Titus the city was taken, and destroyed under circumstances of cruelty and horror without a parallel in the history of the world. No wonder the compassionate Saviour, whose prophetic vision foresaw the dreadful calamities which would fall upon the inhabitants of that devoted city, wept over it, and exclaimed, "Daughters of Jerusalem, weep not for me, but weep for yourselves and for your children." "Behold, your house is left unto you desolate."

The wonderful fulfilment of our Saviour's prophecies respecting the destruction of Jerusalem afford the clearest evidence of the divine character of his mission. "As he was," says Bishop Newton, "the great subject of prophecy, so he was an illustrious prophet himself; and as he excelled in all other spiritual gifts and graces, so was he eminent in this also, and gave ample proofs of his divine commission by his prophecies as well as his miracles."

There were several varieties of coins struck in gold and silver, and in copper and brass, by Vespasian, and by Titus, who succeeded his father on the throne, to commemorate the conquest of Judea and the destruction of Jerusalem. Some of these are mentioned and described by several writers on the subject. One of them is stated to have been issued in the very year of the destruction of Jerusalem; namely, when Vespasian was Consul the third time, in the year of Rome, 823, or A. D. 70.

CHAPTER VI.

Denarius recording the destruction of Jerusalem.

" For the days shall come upon thee, that thine enemies
shall cast a trench about thee, and compass thee round, and
keep thee in on every side, and shall lay thee even with the
ground, and thy children within thee; and they shall not
leave in thee one stone upon another; because thou knewest
not the time of thy visitation." Luke xix. 43, 44.

THE best authorities inform us that the destruction of Jerusalem took place on the 8th
day of September, A. D. 70. There were
also coins issued by Vespasian in A. D. 71,
commemorative of the conquest of Judea, and
in subsequent years during his reign; and
also by Titus, his son, who became Emperor
on the death of his father, A. D. 79. The is-
suing of these coins several years subsequent
to the conquest of that country shows that

the Romans "remembered with pride the subjugation of the rebellious Jews." Writers on the subject of Roman coins describe fifteen varieties, which refer to the conquest of Judea. We present to our readers, with this chapter, a good representation of one of these pieces. It is in the collection of J. Ledyard Hodge, Esqr., of Philadelphia, who has kindly permitted us to make engravings from it. The obverse, or principal side, presents the portrait of the Emperor Vespasian crowned with laurels; his name and titles are inscribed around the coin. The reverse exhibits a female figure seated on the ground at the foot of a trophy, or memorial of victory. Trophies, among the Romans, usually consisted of the arms, shields, helmets, &c., taken from a defeated enemy. The figure of the captive seated on the ground is expressive of the complete subjugation of the country, and the desolation of its inhabitants. It verifies the words of the prophet, "And her gates shall lament and mourn; *and she, being desolate, shall sit upon the ground.*" Isa. iii. 26.

It is not desirable in a brief work of this character, to give the details of the fulfilment of our Lord's predictions respecting the destruction of Jerusalem and of the temple. On this point, and others connected with this interesting subject, we refer our readers to an admirable treatise published by the Presbyterian Board of Publication. The title of this little book (an 18mo., of about 100 pages) is "The destruction of Jerusalem an irresistible proof of the divine origin of Christianity."

We close this chapter with a quotation from its pages. "In executing the command of Titus, relative to the demolition of Jerusalem, the Roman soldiers not only threw down the buildings, but even dug up their foundations, and so completely levelled the whole circuit of the city, that a stranger would scarcely have known that it had ever been inhabited by human beings. Thus was this great city, which, only five months before, had been crowded with nearly two millions of people, who gloried in its impregnable strength, entirely depopulated, and levelled with the ground. And thus also was our Lord's prediction, that her enemies should ' lay her even with the ground,' and 'should not leave in her one stone upon another,' most strikingly and fully accomplished."

CHAPTER VII.

The Mite.

"And there came a certain poor widow, and she threw in two mites." Mark xii. 42.

THE *Lepton*, translated *Mite*, is the lowest denomination of money mentioned in the sacred writings. The precise value of it is a matter of question. But it may with sufficient accuracy be stated to be nearly equal to the one-fifth part of our cent. As the word mite means a very little particle or quantity, so it will be seen by the engraving, which stands at the head of this chapter, that the coin is a very small one. The engraving presents the exact size and appearance of the one in the cabinet of the Mint. This specimen of the mite was found on Mount Ophel, near the site of the ancient temple of Jerusalem. It has but little distinguishing in the

5

marks upon it, except the first letter of the Greek word Λεπτόν, (Lepton). It weighs ten grains.

The lepton, or mite, was a mixture of copper and tin, and was coined by the numerous Greek cities, colonies, and petty states, which were scattered around the Mediterranean sea. The devices or figures upon them, are of various kinds, though, usually the head of a goddess appears upon one side. The one we are considering, we have reason to believe, was coined as long ago as the time when our Saviour was at Jerusalem—" and beheld how the people cast money into the treasury;" and as it was found near the site of the temple, it possesses peculiar interest. It was in the temple where the box was placed to receive the voluntary contributions of the people; and there the poor widow threw in her two mites. The smallness of the offering did not prevent the Saviour from noticing it. On the contrary, he called the special attention of his disciples to her gift, and declared to them, That this poor widow hath cast more in than all they which have cast into the treasury, ver. 43. The reason why our Lord thus commended her offering, appears in the next verse. "For all they did cast in of their abundance; but she of her want did cast in all that she had, even all her living," ver. 44. It is the giving to the cause of Christ, in proportion to our ability, and with a sincere desire to advance his kingdom upon earth, that will render our offerings acceptable to him. We should not despise the day of small things; but make our donations according to the means which Providence has bestowed upon us. Nor should the influence of small contributions be overlooked. When they are brought together they produce important results. As in the natural, so in the moral world.—

> "Little drops of water,
>   Little grains of sand,
>   Make the mighty ocean,
>   And the beauteous land."

> "Little seeds of mercy,
>   Sown by youthful hands,
>   Grow to bless the nations,
>   Far in heathen lands."

CHAPTER VIII.

The Mite.

"This poor widow hath cast more in than all they which have cast into the treasury." Mark xii. 43.

WE have seen in the previous chapter that the mite,—two of which the widow in the text cast into the treasury,—was a very small coin, and of very little value. It would take, for example, *five* hundred of them to make a dollar. We see from this, that it is much less than a cent, for we very well know that *one* hundred cents make a dollar. But the value of money was much greater then than it is now. In a former chapter we stated it to be about ten times greater. We mean by that, to say that a coin equal in value to ten cents, would have bought as much then, as one hundred cents would buy at the present time. The widow's two mites being equal to four mills, would buy as much as four cents would now. Her donation, therefore, may be said to be equal to four cents. It is probable that two mites at that time was a day's wages for a hired woman, and hence they are termed "her living."

The incident we are considering is related by Luke (xxi. 1, &c.,) as well as by Matthew; but neither of the apostles mentions the special purpose to which the contributions received at the temple were applied. Some learned writers are of opinion that they were employed to buy wood for the altar, and other necessaries for the temple, not provided for in any other way. Others suggest that the object was to provide a public fund to be used for charitable purposes. Whether the contributions were to be applied to either or both of these objects, the poor widow exhibited her piety and liberality, by casting into the treasury all that she had to live upon that day, or as the text reads, "even all her living," ver. 44. Christ noticed the gift, and

5 *

graciously commended her for it.   He knew
she did it from pure and good motives; and,
in view of her circumstances, he regarded it
as a greater act of devotion and piety than
the larger contributions of the rich.

The learned Dr. Scott, on this subject observes, that doubtless our Lord saw her heart,
humble and upright, devoted to God, and de-
sirous to express her affection to his worship;
and that she did not cast in her pittance out
of any affectation of singularity, or expecta-
tion of being applauded for it, but depending
on the promises and providences of God, and
out of love to his name.   Others in such circumstances would have pleaded that so small
a sum would be of no use, and that they could
not spare it; and many would have derided
this poor widow, or dissuaded her from making any oblation; but our Lord approved and
commended her conduct; thus teaching us
many important lessons to direct and en-
courage us in our several duties.

We see in this incident that our Lord
watches the treasury, and beholds how the

people cast money therein, ver. 41; and we learn from it that if our donations to the objects of piety and Christian benevolence are made according to our ability, and from proper motives, they will be graciously accepted by him. His requirements extend only to what we have, and not to that which we do not possess.

5 *

CHAPTER IX.

A notice of some money terms used in the Bible, and of coins referred to therein, with their probable value stated in money of the United States.

1. THE SHEKEL is generally put by weight, at half an ounce avoirdupois:—that ounce being composed of four hundred and thirty-seven and a half grains. We adopt, however, the ounce troy of 480 grains in our calculations.

The shekel described in a previous chapter is in a fine state of preservation. It weighs 217 grains, and is of the fineness of 950 thousandths: that is to say, in 1000 parts by weight, 950 are of pure silver, and the remaining part is of an inferior metal or alloy. Other specimens noticed by various authorities make the weight and fineness about the same. The silver coins of the United States, in like manner with most modern nations, are composed of 900 parts of pure silver in every

1000 parts of the metal used in coinage. Reducing the shekel to the standard silver of the United States, the weight of it may properly be stated as equal to 229 grains of that standard. The Mint price of silver is 122 cents 5 mills per ounce. This price was fixed in conformity with the market-price of silver in Europe and in this country, before the recent introduction of a government paper currency, and it affords the best basis upon which to calculate the value of the shekel. At this rate the value of the shekel is 58 cents.

It is proper to notice the fact, that since the year 1853, as authorized by the act of Congress, of March 3, in that year, the silver coins of the United States below the denomination of the dollar are issued at the rate of 125 cents per ounce of standard silver; at that rate the shekel would be worth a little more than 58 cents: but this money being undervalued to keep it in the country, is not a proper rate of value for silver bullion. An under-valuing for a similar purpose, but to a greater extent, is made in English silver money, since the year 1816. We, therefore, put the value of the shekel at 58 cents, as above stated. This was, we have reason to believe, the value of the silver contained in the sacred shekel, or shekel of the sanctuary. The shekel of the King, hereafter to be noticed, was the one-half of the shekel of the sanctuary.

We have been thus particular in stating the value of the shekel, because by it we obtain the unit, from which we can with reasonable certainty state the value of the other money terms used in the sacred Scriptures.

2. THE BEKAH, or half-shekel. This piece of money or coin is sometimes called the royal or profane shekel. The poll-tax paid by the Jews for the support of the tabernacle, and afterward of the temple, and subsequently to the Roman government, was paid in this denomination. The value of the Bekah is 29 cents.

3. THE ZUZA. This piece is not named in the Scriptures, but is put in most of the tables of Jewish money. It was the fourth part

of a shekel, and is referred to in 1 Samuel, ix. 8. Value, 14 cents and 5 mills.

4. THE GERAH. The twentieth part of a shekel. Value, 2 cents and 9 mills.

5. THE MANEH. This term was used for silver as well as gold. The weight of it was equal to sixty shekels: therefore, the *maneh of silver* was of the value of $34.80.

Writers usually arrive at the value of ancient gold and silver coins and money terms, by adopting the proportion between these metals as used in modern times. This proportion in Europe and America, is about sixteen to one; and the tables of the values of ancient coins in our Bibles and commentaries are fixed upon that ratio. But that proportion over-states the value of gold among the Jews and the neighbouring nations. From a careful examination of the various authorities on this subject, we have reason to believe that at the periods when the money-terms of the Bible were used, the proportion between the values of gold

and silver was as ten to one: that is to
say, one ounce of gold was worth as much
as ten ounces of silver. Adopting this
proportion, the *maneh of gold* was worth
$348.00.

CHAPTER X.

The Talent.

THE weight of the Jewish talent was equal to 3000 shekels. The shekel, as we have shown, weighed 217 grains: consequently the talent weighed 651,000 grains, equal to 93 lbs. avoirdupois.

Talent, as a money-term, was used for silver and gold.

Assuming the silver to be of the fineness of the shekel, and thus being "current with the merchant," the value of the talent of silver may be put at the sum of $1740.

The talent of gold, according to the ratio heretofore noticed, was therefore worth $17,400.

THE GREEK TALENT, usually was of the weight of 6000 drachms or drams. The weight of the dram was 60 grains, being the eighth part of the ounce of 480 grains, it was therefore of the weight of 51 lbs. 6 oz. 5 dwt.,

6

avoirdupois.   At the rate of fineness herein-
before stated, namely, 950 thousandths, the
dram of silver was worth 16 cents : the *Greek
Talent of silver* may therefore be put at
$960.00.   Following the proportion, that
one talent of gold was equal to ten talents
of silver, the *Greek Talent* of gold was
$9,600.00.

A talent was two-fold, namely, to express
a weight, or a sum of money.   The value of
it differed according to the different ages and
countries in which it was used.   In the Old
Testament the talent referred to, with perhaps one or two exceptions, which will be
noticed, is the Jewish talent of 3000 shekels.

Thus the golden candlestick with the tongs
and the snuff-dishes for the tabernacle, was
to be made of a talent of gold; this was of
the weight of 93 pounds; and was of the
value of $17,400.   Exodus xxv. 39.   The
amount of gold employed in the tabernacle,
was 29 talents and seven hundred and thirty
shekels; the value of which was $508,834.00;
of silver there was used 100 talents and 1775

shekels, equal to $175,029.50. Exodus xxxviii. 24, 25.

The silver above named, was contributed by 603,550 men, who each paid a half-shekel, as required in Exodus xxx. 13, 14. And it is from the enumeration and statement in Exodus xxxviii. 24, 25, 26, we ascertain that the talent contained 3000 shekels.

King Hiram sent to king Solomon 120 talents, ($2,088,000.) 1 Kings ix. 14.

Solomon brought from Ophir 420 talents, ($7,308,000.) 1 Kings ix. 28.

The Queen of Sheba gave Solomon 120 talents, ($2,088,000.) 1 Kings x. 10.

The weight of the gold that came to Solomon in one year, was 666 talents, ($11,588,400.) 1 Kings x. 14.

The temple of Solomon was overlaid with gold, amounting to 600 talents, ($10,440,000.) 2 Chron. iii. 8.

We need not multiply these examples; the reader can readily, by the data given, convert the term *talent*, where it occurs in the Bible, into the money of the United States.

CHAPTER XI.

The Talent—Continued.

THERE was another talent however, of great antiquity, which some authorities call the *Homerical talent.* It is believed to have been used by the Phœnicians. This talent is mentioned by Homer in such a manner as to show that it was of greatly inferior value to the talents we have been considering.* Some authorities conjecture that it was equivalent in value to some correspondent talent in brass; the value of the brass rating as 1 to 100, as compared with silver, and the latter as 1 to 10 compared with gold. It is probably according to this ancient talent that the statement is made in 1 Chron. xxii. 14, where it is said that king David had "provided for the temple 100,000 talents of gold, and one thousand thousand talents of silver." Josephus, referring to this passage, states the

* See note 4, page 82.

amount as 10,000 talents of gold, and 100,000 of silver. Dr. Scott, in his commentary, speaking of the enormous amount indicated by the usual reading of the text in question, observes, "It is generally concluded either that some mistake has taken place in the numerical letters, or that a talent of inferior weight and value is meant."

Dr. Jenks, on the same text says, "I am inclined to suppose that a certain number is here put for an uncertain number, because it is said in ver. 16, that of the gold and silver as well as of brass and iron, there was no number." By this view, the talent may here be said to be used to express a large and indefinite amount, in like manner as the terms thousands and tens of thousands are often used by us without reference to any precise number.

Dr. Arbuthnot, a learned writer, on ancient coins, on the same text says, "David reigned in Judea after the siege of Troy, so that it is no ways improbable but Homer and he might use the same talent." Dr. Anthon,

6 *

speaking of a small talent, which was probably the same to which we refer, says, "It was called the Sicilian talent, from being much used by the Greeks of Italy and Sicily," and adds, "This small talent explains the use of the term great talent (Magnum talentum) which we find in Latin authors; for the Attic talent was great in comparison with this."

From data gathered from several authorities, this talent was probably of the weight of twenty-four drachmas, equal to three troy ounces; putting the silver at the standard fineness heretofore given, the value of this talent of silver was about $3.88; and $38. 80, for the talent of gold. At this rate of valuation, king David gathered together "in his trouble," or in his poverty, as it may be rendered, $7,760,000; comprised in equal amounts of gold and silver.

The same talent is probably referred to in 1 Chron. xxix. 4–7. This opinion is strengthened by the fact that the term *dram* is there used: if it had been the Jewish talent, and there were parts of the talent to be expressed, no doubt it would be stated in *shekels*, as is done in Exodus xxxviii. 24, 25.

As the usual reading of these parts of Scripture give an imperfect idea of the values intended to be expressed, we have deemed it proper to present our views somewhat at large upon the subject.

Where the word talent occurs as a term of money, in other parts of the Old Testament, the value may be taken to be the Jewish talent of 3000 shekels; and in the New Testament, the Greek talent of 6000 drams.*

* See note 5, page 83.

CHAPTER XII.

A general statement of the Coins and Money-terms of the Bible; with Tables of their Weight and Value.

IT is now the general custom in Europe, as well as in America, to express the weight of gold and silver in the ounce troy, and its decimal fractions. The Mint of the United States has for many years adopted that system in the mode of weighing and keeping accounts; thus getting rid of the inconvenience which arises from the use of penny-weights and grains. At a later period, the same mode was adopted by the Bank and Mint of England. The fineness of gold and silver is now generally expressed by the term thousandths, adopting a form introduced by French assayers.

In the tables herein presented, the weights are expressed in the troy ounce, and its decimal fractions, carrying it to the third figure, namely, thousandths of an ounce. For the reason that most of our readers are doubtless accustomed to estimate and calculate weights by the avoirdupois pound, and its subdivisions, we also state the weights according to that system.

In calculating the *value* of the coins and money terms, we use the troy ounce, (480 grains.) Silver is valued at $1.22 cts. 5 mills per ounce of standard fineness. This standard, as authorized by the laws of the United States, is so constituted that of 1000 parts by weight, 900 are of pure silver, and 100 of copper. The valuation per ounce, accords very nearly with the price of silver of like fineness at London and Paris, by whose markets the value of silver throughout the world is regulated.

The value of gold is rated in the proportion of ten to one of silver, for the reasons stated in a previous chapter.

* See note 6, page 87.

CHAPTER XIII.

The Parable of the Talents.

Matthew xxv. 14 to 30.

IN previous chapters we have noticed the talent as a weight, and as expressive of a sum of money; and also that it differed in value in the several countries in which it was used. But the term talent is now used in our language as a metaphor to indicate a quality of the mind, namely, ability, capacity, gift or faculty. For this use of the word talent (*talenton*) we are indebted to the parable of our Lord as recorded in the 25th chapter of the Gospel by Matthew. This parable gives a spiritual significance to the word. "The kingdom of heaven is as a man travelling into a far country, who called his own servants and delivered unto them his goods," verse 14. The goods were talents. The master and owner delivered them to his servants, (*doulos*—slaves,) to increase them in his absence. "Slaves in antiquity were often artisans, or were allowed otherwise to engage freely in business, paying, as it was frequently arranged, a fixed yearly sum to their masters: or, as here, they had money given them wherewith to trade on his account, or with which to enlarge their business, and to bring him in a share of their profits."[1]

The talents given to the servants were not equally distributed. "Unto one he gave five talents, to another two, and to another one; to every man according to his several ability," v. 15.

There is a difference in the amount of these gifts; and yet it is to be observed that each of the servants received *one talent* from the master. The one to whom the least was given was the most faulty: perhaps to teach

---

[1] Trench on the Parables, p. 221, referring to Greswell's Explanation of the Parables; and Dictionary of Grecian and Roman Ant., title *Servus*.

us that such an one might be inclined to say what signifies the *little* whether it be done or left undone. We are instructed that the Lord looks for fidelity in little as well as in much. But in fact the talent represents a large sum of money, whether we take the Jewish talent of the Old Testament, or the Greek talent of the New Testament. No word was then in use to express a greater weight or value. In like manner, the trust or charge committed to every individual in Christ's spiritual kingdom is of great value, and cannot be over-estimated.

This parable teaches that mankind are the subjects of God's government, and are responsible to him for the exercise of the talents or ability which he has bestowed upon them. Every one is required to be faithful in the service or duty which Providence places before him. "Whatsoever thy hand findeth to do, do it with thy might." Do this, whether it involves the use of one talent or of many; whether the occasion or duty is great or small. It will surely be no defence for any one to say that his gift or ability is less than another's. Let every one endeavour, through the assistance of divine grace, to improve the talent given to him, and thus promote his own true and substantial happiness, and that of others within the influence of his example.

In the parable before us, two of the servants were diligent and active in the use of the talents committed to their charge. They regarded them not only as a valuable manifestation of the kindness and confidence of their master, but as a sacred trust committed to them. As stewards or trustees, they felt bound to a faithful and active use of the means which were placed in their hands, and that it was not reasonable or proper that so much money or ability should remain unemployed or idle. They were faithful servants; and each one received the plaudit, "Well done, good and faithful servant, thou hast been faithful over a few things, I will make thee ruler over many things : enter thou into the joy of thy lord." What that joy shall be, who can tell? Even an inspired Apostle

7

exclaims, "Eye hath not seen, nor ear heard, neither have entered into the heart of man, the things which God hath prepared for them that love him."

Within the mansions prepared by the Bridegroom is light, happiness, and sacred joy. There his faithful servants shall see his face and his name shall be written on their foreheads. "Blessed are they which are called to the marriage supper of the Lamb." It is but little that we can receive here ; some drops of joy that enter *into us ;* but there we shall enter into joy, as vessels put into a sea of happiness.

One of the servants in the parable was unfaithful. He neglected to improve the talent committed to his charge. He did not spend it in riotous living like the Prodigal son, but he hid it in the earth like a miser. It is no uncommon thing for men to hide money of silver and gold in the earth; and sometimes in cellars and under hearth-stones. This practice is induced not only from a mean and miserly disposition, but from a want of confidence in others, and in the monied institutions of the country. Besides the wrong to society at large which such a practice produces, it often leads to great personal injury to those who adopt it. Instances of robbery, and even murder, are not unfrequent where such hoarding of treasure is known to exist. Thus even in a temporal point of view the hiding of treasure in the earth is productive of evil, and is injurious in its consequences.

The unfaithful servant took a false view of the character of the master. He entirely overlooked his grace in entrusting him with such a considerable sum as a talent; and that too without any security; thus giving him the opportunity of advancing the interests of his master, as well as his own, by the use of the money in the usual course of lawful business. He ought to have known that the master desired the talent to be used and improved. If such had not been his intention he could as well have let it lie idle and unemployed, as could the servant. The fact of giving it to the servant, in the manner mentioned in the parable, shows that the intention of the master was, that the talent should be used as money, and not hid in the cellar, or in the field or garden, or under a hearth-stone.

When he was called upon to render an account of his stewardship it is no wonder he was afraid. In his confusion and trepidation he confessed his offence; and even admitted the hard thoughts he entertained of his master—showing that he either had neglected to give the subject a proper consideration, or had wilfully misunderstood his master's expectations, or negligently omitted to comply with them. He should have had such confidence in his master that even if he had lost the money, or a part of it, in an honest and faithful effort to increase it, when his judgment only was at fault, he might nevertheless have thrown himself upon the compassion and mercy of his master, and by repentance and submission ask and obtain his pardon and forgiveness. But no, he called the service a hard service, even when he did nothing but dig a hole in the earth and hide the talent therein. The master pronounces him "a wicked and slothful servant;" and referring to the plea which the servant makes, namely, that he was "a hard man," he adds, "Thou oughtest therefore to have put my money to the exchangers; and then at my coming I should have received mine own with usury." In other words, if he was afraid of using the money in the ordinary way of business, he might at least have deposited it with a banker who would have allowed an increase, or interest thereon.

The word *usura*, from whence comes our modern term usury, signifies a price for the *use* of any thing. The word is now understood to mean the taking of *more* than lawful interest. It may be here noted that interest, or a price for the use of money, was forbidden among the Jews, and also among the Romans, by an old law of that Republic. But neither Jews nor Romans were forbidden to take interest from strangers, that is to say, from those who were not of their own nation or people. The servant therefore clearly neglected his duty in both aspects of the case, namely, 1. In omitting to apply his talent in some useful business. 2. In not depositing it with a banker, or exchanger, who would have allowed interest for its use.

The neglect to improve the talent, or to put it out to the exchangers, by which a lawful return in interest might have been secured, was attended with disastrous consequences to the unfaithful servant. The talent was taken from him who had thus made a bad use of it, and given to the servant who had gained five talents as a reward for his industry and fidelity. But this was not all; he was condemned as an unprofitable servant and "cast into outer darkness." There is light and joy *in* the house when the bridegroom cometh. "Blessed are they that do his commandments that they may have right to the tree of life, and may enter through the gates into the city." But those who are without, when the door is shut, will be left in darkness, gloom, and despair.

May none of my readers be among the unhappy number of those who misapply the talents which are bestowed upon them, or "bury them in the earth;" but may they, through the abundant goodness of God, be enabled to so employ their time, their money, and their abilities, as to receive the welcome plaudit, "Well done, good and faithful servant; thou hast been faithful over a few things, I will make thee ruler over many things, enter thou into the joy of thy Lord."

THE CHILD'S TALENT.

God entrusts to all
    Talents few or many;
None so young and small
    That they have not any.

Though the great and wise
    Have a greater number,
Yet my one I prize,
    And it must not slumber.

God will surely ask,
    Ere I enter heaven,
Have I done the task
    Which to me was given?

Little drops of rain
   Bring the springing flowers,
And I may attain
   Much by little powers.

Every little mite,
   Every little measure,
Helps to spread the light,
   Helps to swell the treasure.

Note 1. (Page 8.)

It is proper to note, in connexion with what is said in the introductory chapter, that the Hebrew word *Kesitoth*, sometimes translated "pieces of money," and "pieces of silver," has some reference to the value of a *lamb*. As in Genesis xxxiii. 19, where it is recorded that for a hundred "*pieces of money*," Jacob bought a parcel of a field, where he had pitched his tent, and on which he erected an altar to the God of Israel. The same purchase is referred to in Joshua xxiv. 32, where it is also rendered "pieces of silver." And in Job xlii. 11, where it is said "every man also gave him a piece of money," (*Kesitah*, singular of Kesitoth.) At an early, and perhaps contemporaneous period, as we learn from ancient inscriptions from time to time brought to light through the investigations of antiquarians, the Egyptians used weights the *form* of which was that of a *lamb*. This was used in weighing gold and silver, and we are of opinion, adopting the best authorities on the subject, that they had reference to the value of a lamb in these metals. We do not therefore concur with those commentators of the Bible who state that the pieces mentioned in the above cited texts had the impression of a lamb upon them; on the contrary, we think that they represented an amount of the precious metals which was the adopted or commercial value of a lamb.

The *just weight* of the pieces of silver was determined by the scales or balances. In the marginal references to the texts we have cited, the word *lamb* or *lambs* is used.

Note 2. (Page 18.)

COINS are the most enduring and important memorials of ancient history. In several instances they have supplied materials of his-

tory which otherwise would have been lost.
Ancient coins are well preserved, and are re-
produced from time to time, from several
causes and considerations. 1. Because, they
were generally composed of metals the least
destructible, namely, gold and silver. 2. The
insecurity of property among most ancient
nations induced the practice of acquiring the
least bulky, and the most readily secreted
treasure, namely, coins. 3. Such hoarding
of treasure was often made by burying it in
the earth, in fields, in gardens, and under
houses, after it was carefully placed in jars
and pots. 4. In subsequent ages, and in our
own times, these treasures have been dug up
and thus found.

The learned theologian and orientalist, Dr.
Michaelis, says, " It is sufficient, in answer to
the question, Is the New Testament ancient
and genuine? to reply, compare it with the
history of the times, and you cannot doubt of
its authenticity."

Note 3. (Page 28.)

THE word *Stater* (στατήρ) signifies standard. The coin was adjusted to some well-
known and established standard. This standard of gold appears to have been a weight
corresponding to two drachmæ of silver, and
of the value of twenty in silver. (Hum-
phrey's Man., vol. 1, p. 10.) This valuation
of gold compared with silver corroborates the
proportionate value of these two metals during and near the period when the money terms
of the Bible were used, as we have shown at
page 57 of this book.

Note 4. (Page 62.)

HOMER states that at the funeral of Patro-
clus the prizes were in the following order. 1.
A captive woman and a tripod. 2. A mare
and colt. 3. A kettle. 4. Two talents of
gold. 5. A brass bowl, or urn.

Eustathius, archbishop of Thessalonica, who was deeply read in the classics, and one of the most learned men of his time, in his commentaries upon Homer, written about A. D. 1160, reckons the Homerical talent as equal only to twenty-four drachms, or three troy ounces.

The exchange of armours referred to at page 8, between the heroes Glaucus and Diomed, is thus translated by Pope.

" For Diomed's brass arms of mean device
   For which nine oxen paid, (a vulgar price,)
   He[1] gave his own of gold divinely wrought,
   A hundred beeves the shining purchase brought."

Note 5. (Page 65.)

THE propriety of the valuation of the talent we have herein given will be apparent when we consider how enormous the sums mentioned in 1 Chron. xxii. 14, would be,

[1] Glaucus.

if either the Jewish talent of 3,000 shekels, or the Greek talent of 6,000 drachms, was intended. If we take the former, the amount King David had provided would appear to be in gold 1740 millions of dollars; and a similar amount in silver; making in the aggregate the sum of 2480 millions of dollars. If we suppose the Greek talent was intended, the sums would make 1920 millions of dollars. These sums are so enormous as to be utterly incredible. And yet some writers have supposed that the ordinary talent of Scripture was intended in these passages. Others, more considerately, have conjectured that some error has crept into the sacred text. The explanation and views herein given renders it highly probable, if not reasonably certain, that an inferior talent was used. This conclusion is also strengthened by the consideration that David and Solomon, particularly the latter, carried on quite an extensive commerce and intercourse with the adjacent, and some of the distant countries of Asia and Europe; it would be reasonable and appropriate that the wealth which had been collected and expended in the erection and adornment of the Temple should be expressed in terms that would be properly understood by other nations, and particularly by the Phœnicians, with whom they had a constant intercourse.

Adopting this inferior talent, namely, the talent of twenty-four drachms, equal to three troy ounces, as the one intended in 1 Chronicles, the sums mentioned are reasonable and probable. "One hundred thousand talents of gold" was equal to three millions eight hundred and eighty-eight thousand dollars, money of the United States; and "a thousand thousand talents of silver," (a million of talents) were equal to a like sum of three millions eight hundred and eighty-eight thousand dollars; making in the aggregate the sum of seven millions seven hundred and sixty thousand dollars.

The donation by King David, and the contributions of the people, recorded in 1 Chron. xxix. 4th to 7th verses included, were made *after* the principal sum above mentioned had been collected and provided for the building of the Temple. The king's gift in gold was of the value of one hundred and forty-six thousand four hundred dollars; and in silver, twenty-seven thousand one hundred and sixty dollars. The "princes, captains, and rulers," gave in gold one hundred and ninety-four thousand and sixty-five dollars, and in silver, thirty-eight thousand eight hundred dollars. Total amount of contributions in gold and silver, four hundred and six thousand, four hundred and twenty-five dollars, ($406,425.) The princes and rulers also gave large quantities of "brass" and "iron" for the building of the Temple, and "precious stones," to adorn it, and the vestments of the priests, the value of which it is, in this connexion, unnecessary to consider, even if we had any reliable information on the subject, which in fact we have not.

These generous contributions, we learn from the inspired record, were freely and willingly offered. "Then the people rejoiced because with perfect heart they offered willingly to the Lord: and David the king also rejoiced with great joy." This interesting transaction affords a striking instance of the liberality and zeal of God's people, and is worthy of imitation in all ages.

Note 6. (Page 67.)

THE author has received numerous testimonials of the value and accuracy of the statements and tables in this little work. It is deemed proper to insert one of these testimonials, inasmuch as it emanates from a gentleman who is very well informed on the subject of ancient and modern coins. Referring to the first edition, sent to him by the author, he says, "Accept my thanks for a copy of 'The Coins of the Bible, and its money terms.' Agreeably to your polite and friendly request, I have examined the statements of fact in your work, and they appear to me to be

8 *

carefully made, and reliable. As a manual of reference the book will always be useful.

"As the *talent* and the *pound* were monies of account, and not coins, I have not heretofore given much attention to them. The parable of the ten pounds (*deka mnai*) in Luke xix. gives an interest to the mina or maneh. It evidently, as you state, represented 100 drachms in the Greek system.

"In speaking of the value of the 'penny' of that day, and of its being the measure of a day's work, it might have been well to say, that to this day the same amount of silver goes quite as far, or farther in the region of Syria. In Switzerland, a day's labour is about 15 cents; in Ireland not long since about 20 cents. So that it is very necessary to correct the Sunday scholar's ideas, and others, about the price paid for labour, and the liberality of the good Samaritan; and to show the difference between the working-man here, and over there, down to our own times.

"The relation of gold to silver, in ancient times, is a very interesting subject. Knowing that Prof. J. II. Alexander of Baltimore, one of the most learned and accurate scholars of our day, had thoroughly examined that subject, I wrote to him, and have received a full and satisfactory reply. In effect, he concludes by accepting the authority of Boeckh, saying,—'I think the ratio he (B.) takes, namely ten to one, to be reasonably well established, as common for several centuries before and after the Christian era.' This is a confirmation of your view."[1]

[1] Letter from W. E. Dubois, Esq., Assistant Assayer U. S. Mint.

A Table of Jewish Weights.

	lbs.	oz.	dwt.	grs.
Shekel, 217 grs.=0 oz. 452 dec. or			9	1
Maneh, (60 shekels) 13,020 grs.=27 oz. 125 dec. or	1	1	5	20
Talent, (3000 shekels) 651,000 grs.=1356 oz. 458 dec.	93	0	0	0

Greek (Attic) Weights.

Drachma, 60 grs.=to 0 oz. 125 dec. or			2	12
Mina, (100 drachmas) 6000 grs. =125 oz. or		12	10	0
Talent, (6000 drachmas) 360,000 grs.= 750 oz. or	51	6	5	0

A Table of Jewish Coins and Money-terms.

	ct. m.
Gerah, one-twentieth of a shekel,	2.9
Zuzah, one-fourth of a shekel,	14.5
Bekah, shekel of the king, or half-shekel,	29
Shekel of silver,	58
Shekel of gold,	$5.80
Maneh of silver, (60 shekels)	$34.80
Maneh of gold, " "	$348.00
Talent of silver, (3000 shekels)	$1740.00
Talent of gold, " "	$17,400.00

Greek (Attic) Coins and Money-terms.

	ct. m.
Lepton, (Mite,)	0.2
Obolus,	2.6

	ct. m.
Drachm, "piece of silver," Luke xv. 8.	16.0
Didrachm,	32.0
Tetradrachm (or stater)	64.0
Mina (100 drachms) of silver, "pound." Luke xix. 13.	$16.00
Mina, (100 drachms,) of gold,	$160.00
Talent, (6000 drachms) of silver,	$960.00
Talent, " " of gold,	$9600.00

ROMAN COINS.

	cts. m.
Assarius, one-tenth part of the denarius ("farthing." Matt. x. 29.)	1.5
Quadrans, (or Sestertius) one-fourth of the denarius ("farthing." Matt. v. 26.)	3.75
Quinarius, half denarius.	7.5
Denarius, ("Penny." Matt. xx. 2; xxii. 19, &c.)	15.0
Aureus, (stater) Gold coin, weighed double the denarius, value,	$3.00

The Romans usually reckoned money by *Sestertii*. For example, the sum of 1000 *Sestertii* was called *Sestertium*, &c.

		cts. m.
1	*Sestertius*	3.75
10	*Sestertii*	37.5
100	"	$3.75
1000	"	$37.50

Their use of the word *talent*, as a money term, is not very exact. The Roman talent, however, as a weight, was equal to 60 libræ or pounds; the pound being divided into 12 ounces. According to the rate and proportion herein given, the Roman talent of silver may be valued at $931.00
The talent of gold, $9310.00

The denarius during the time of the Commonwealth is

generally put as equal to the drachm (16 cents,) but it was of diminished weight during the Empire. In the time of the New Testament it may be valued, as above stated, at 15 cents.

In the Old Testament, where the term "piece of money," is used in our translation, the word "*shekel*" generally occurs in the original text. In the New Testament, *drachma* is translated "piece of silver," Luke xv. 8. And *argurion*, "pieces of silver," Matt. xxvi. 15; Matt. xxvii. 6–9; Acts xix. 19. *Argurion*, "money," Matt. xxv. 18–27; Luke xix. 23. *Didrachma*, "tribute" (money.) Matt. xvii. 24.

Talent, Homerical or Phœnician.

| Gold, | " | " | $38.80 |
| Silver, | " | " | $3.88 |

ALPHABETICAL INDEX.